The Twelve Teas® of Celebration

EMILIE BARNES

Paintings by
SUSAN RIOS

HARVEST HOUSE PUBLISHERS

EUGENE, OREGON

THE TWELVE TEAS® OF CELEBRATION

Text copyright © 2003 by Harvest House Publishers
Published by Harvest House Publishers
Eugene, Oregon 97402
www.harvesthousepublishers.com

Library of Congress Cataloging-in-Publication Data

Barnes, Emilie.
  The twelve teas of celebration / text by Emilie Barnes ; paintings by
Susan Rios.
     p. cm.
  ISBN-13: 978-0-7369-1067-5
  ISBN-10: 0-7369-1067-0 (alk. paper)
  1. Afternoon teas. 2. Tea. 3. Entertaining. I. Rios, Susan. II. Title.
  TX736.B374 2003
  641.5'3--dc21

                                   2003001824

Original artwork copyright © Susan Rios. Licensed by Art Impressions, Canoga Park, CA. For more information
about Susan Rios, please contact:

          Susan Rios Incorporated
          15335 Morrison St., Suite 102
          Sherman Oaks, CA 91403
          www.susanriosinc.com

THE TWELVE TEAS is a registered trademark of The Hawkins Children's LLC. Harvest House Publishers, Inc.,
is the exclusive licensee of the federally registered trademark THE TWELVE TEAS.

Design and production by Garborg Design Works, Minneapolis, Minnesota

Unless otherwise indicated, verses are taken from the Holy Bible: New International Version®. NIV®. Copyright
© 1973, 1978, 1984 by the International Bible Society. Used by permission of Zondervan Publishing House.

Verses marked TEV are taken from the Today's English Version - Second Edition Copyright © 1992 by American
Bible Society. Used by permission.

Verses marked NASB are taken from the New American Standard Bible®, © 1960, 1962, 1963, 1968, 1971, 1972,
1973, 1975, 1977, 1995 by The Lockman Foundation. Used by permission.

Printed in Hong Kong.

07 08 09 / NG / 7 6 5